RESURRECTIONS
IN THE SEASON OF THE LONGEST DROUGHT

*They asked for ancestors, for illustrious ancestors,
and I said to Forest Head, let me answer their request.
And I sent two spirits of the restless dead . . .*

Wole Soyinka

'BIYI BANDELE-THOMAS

RESURRECTIONS
IN THE SEASON OF THE LONGEST DROUGHT

AMBER LANE PRESS

All rights whatsoever in this play are strictly reserved and application for performance, etc. must be made before rehearsals begin to:
Curtis Brown
162-168 Regent Street
London W1R 5TB

No performance may be given unless a licence has been obtained.

First published in 1994 by
Amber Lane Press Ltd,
Cheorl House, Church Street,
Charlbury, Oxford OX7 3PR
Telephone: 0608 810024

Printed in Great Britain by
Bocardo Press Ltd, Didcot, Oxon.

Copyright © 'Biyi Bandele-Thomas, 1994

The right of 'Biyi Bandele-Thomas to be identified as author of this work has been asserted by him in accordance with Section 77 of the Copyright, Designs and Patents Act 1988.

ISBN 1 872868 13 4

CONDITIONS OF SALE

This book is sold subject to the condition that it shall not, by way of trade or otherwise, be lent, re-sold, hired out or otherwise circulated without the publisher's prior consent in any form of binding or cover other than that in which it is published and without a similar condition including this condition being imposed on the subsequent purchaser.

Characters

BB ... early to mid-30s
MEBUDE ... mid-20s
SANTANA ... BB's gatekeeper-cum-watchman, early 20s
YINKA ... A friend of BB's, early to mid-30s
ADAMA ... BB's lawyer, mid-30s
JUDGE BASSEY ... late 50s
INSPECTOR KAMORU ... late 50s
OLD MAN ... Santana's late grandfather, old but alert
OLD WOMAN ... Yinka's late mother
DOCTOR
MAN
BEGGARS
POLICE / SECURITY / SOLDIERS
TOWNSPEOPLE

The action takes place in Lagos, Nigeria in the mid-1908s.

Resurrections was given a rehearsed reading, in an earlier draft, at the Royal Court Theatre Upstairs, London on 5th February 1993. It was directed by Annie Castledine with the following cast:

SANTANA..........Susan Aderin
JUDGE BASSEY..........Jude Akuwudike
ADAMA..........Pauline Black
INSPECTOR KAMORU..........Femi Elufowoju, Jr.
BB..........Patrice Naiambana
MEBUDE..........Pamela Nomvete
YINKA..........Leo Wringer

All other parts played by members of the company

It was subsequently workshopped and given a rehearsed reading at New Dramatists, Manhattan, New York on 22nd May 1993. It was directed by Clinton Turner Davis with the following cast:

JUDGE BASSEY..........David Fonteno
BEGGAR 2 / PRESS 2..........Hazelle Goodman
SANTANA..........Tony Haney
INSPECTOR KAMORU..........Jonathan Earl Peck
ADAMA..........Kimi Sung
BB..........Raymond Anthony Thomas
YINKA..........Chris Walker
MEBUDE..........Felicia Wilson

All other parts played by members of the company

Resurrections was among 15 plays selected from over 900 entries for the New Work Festival, Los Angeles in 1994 and was given a rehearsed reading at the Mark Taper Forum on 3rd February 1994. It was directed by Timothy Douglas with the following cast:

MEBUDE..........Angela Bassett
SANTANA..........Bruce Beatty
INSPECTOR KAMORU..........Bill Cobbs
JUDGE BASSEY..........John Cothran, Jr.
YINKA..........Brent Jennings
BB..........Carl Lumbly
ADAMA..........Lorraine Toussaint
BEGGAR 2 / PRESS 2..........Gregory Wallace

All other parts played by members of the company

The first full-scale production of *Resurrections* was given by Talawa Theatre Company at the Cochrane Theatre, London on 3rd October 1994. It was directed by Yvonne Brewster with the following cast:

YINKA............David Carr
BEGGAR 2..........Antonia Coker
BEGGAR 1..........Femi Elufowoju, Jr.
ADAMA..........Glenna Forster-Jones
BEGGAR 3..........Ganiat Kasumu
INSPECTOR KAMORU..........Trevor Laird
SANTANA..........Colin McFarlane
BB..........Ben Thomas
JUDGE BASSEY..........Don Warrington
MEBUDE..........Angela Wynter

Designer..........Ellen Cairns
Lighting by Richard Moffatt
Choreography by Greta Mendez

Prologue

ONCE UPON A KING

Late evening.

The front entrance of the residence of BIKAN BABAR-INSA (BB) *in downtown Lagos Mainland.*

There is a fence around the house. Within this fence, by a swing gate, is a small shed, tortured out from corrugated iron sheets.

A hurricane lantern glows feebly from a wall. The stooped figure of SANTANA, *the gatekeeper-cum-watchman, is clearly visible even in the darkness. He is leaning against the wall of his shed, a shakabula* rifle propped between his shoulders like a Fulani cattle rearer's herding stick. The only indication that he is awake is the constant movement of his hands to ward off mosquitos.*

BB's *arrival is heralded by the horde of* BEGGARS *who follow fast on his heels.*

BEGGARS [*off*] For di Baba ke!

BEGGAR 1 [*off*] Baba BB,
Husband of my mother,
My sister's secret lover,
I'm yours too; step on me,
I'm your honoured mat,
Unroll me to the path of fame!

BEGGARS [*off*] For di Baba ke!

BEGGAR 2 [*off*] The only man who crossed
the River Niger on a bicycle;

---

* Dane gun

And crossed the desert for a dare.
You who beckoned to a passing *aeromplane*
And it stopped and offered you a lift.

> [BB *appears from the shadows. He is gloriously tipsy. The* BEGGARS *follow.* BEGGAR 1 *is male,* BEGGAR 2 *and* BEGGAR 3 *are female.*]

BEGGAR 1   Kill me!
Skin me!
Turn me into that pair of exotic sandals on your feet: walk me to the house of wealth!

BEGGARS   For di Baba ke.

> [*singing*] O baa takiti
> Kio f'ori so le
> Baba ni Baba nje! *

> [BB *is quite enjoying this but pretends to be irritated.*]

BB   Out of my way, you little crooks. Get out of my way!

BEGGAR 3   May you live longer than Nebuchadnezzar.

BEGGAR 1   May you service more brides in one day than King Solomon ever did in his lifetime.

BEGGAR 2   May your okra always draw.

BEGGAR 3   May it always be hot and spicy
So when Madam tastes it at night.

BEGGAR 2   Or first thing in the morning
For that special start to the day.

BEGGAR 1   When she tastes it, and it goes into her, she'll cry as always...

BEGGARS   Fire de for my body!

BB   You cheeky prats.

---

* It doesn't matter what you do / Convulse in envy / Keel over with jealousy / The Boss remains the Boss.

PROLOGUE

BEGGAR 2 May your loins be gifted...

BEGGAR 1 Not only so you could create that dream football team...

BEGGAR 3 And the other eleven they'll be playing against...

BEGGAR 1 But also the spectators watching through the keyhole.

   [SANTANA *comes out of his shed, unslings his gun and takes aim.*]

SANTANA I have tell you plenty time not to be disturb my master.

   [*The* BEGGARS *immediately turn on him.*]

BEGGAR 2 Poor man too foolish o!

BEGGAR 1 Crayfish-head.

BEGGAR 2 Go wash your mouth, my brother. Dirty mouth cannot talk clean thing.

   [SANTANA *holds the gun threateningly.*]

BEGGAR 3 Leave di poor man alone: he fit to be say he never touch woman for ten years.

BEGGAR 2 Poor man! Him body don full.

SANTANA [*to* BB] Make you warn dem o, master, warn dem before I vex too much o.

BB Leave the fellow alone, you rascals.

   [*As if by rehearsed agreement, the* BEGGARS *swing round and face* BB, *proffering their upturned caps and hats in anticipation of being paid to leave* SANTANA *alone.* BB *dips his hands into his gown and pulls out a fistful of naira notes, which he proceeds to fling carelessly at the* BEGGARS.]

Off with you lot.

   [*As they run back to the street the* BEGGARS *give parting thanks.*]

BEGGAR 2 May it never finish, where this comes from...

BEGGAR 1   May *they* always arrive only after you've left...

BEGGAR 3   Day and night, that's you and the law!

BEGGARS   For di Baba ke!

> [*The* BEGGARS *make rude noises at* SANTANA *and leave.*]

BB   [*to* BEGGAR 1] May you walk around with a permanent erection!

SANTANA   [*full of reproach*] Is bad to be opening teeth with dem like dat, sah. Small time now dem no go know dem place.

BB   Have the guests started to arrive?

SANTANA   Yessah. Dem don de come small-small.

BB   Good. And the band?

SANTANA   Those ones? Dem useless too much. Dem jus' de come.

BB   Good.

SANTANA   Wetin good for there, sah?

> [BB *dips into his gown. Obviously they are not operating on the same wavelength.*]

BB   Good. Are you alright, then?

SANTANA   Mesef? [*shrugs*] Anyway, we thank God.

> [BB *brings out a whole wad of naira notes and flings them at* SANTANA.]

BB   Keep it.

> [*He heads for the door to go into the house.*]

SANTANA   Sah?

BB   I've been poor and I've been rich. Rich is better.

SANTANA   I don't understand at all.

BB   Hold on to the change, young man.

> [*Pause.*]

SANTANA   God bless you, sah.

Act One

ALL HAIL THE KING

Scene One

Later that night, in front of BB's house.

The door swings open. A flood of light from inside washes over the front porch, and with it music crashes out. Party noises.

MEBUDE comes running out through the door. She stands on the porch, gasping for air.

SANTANA comes out from the shadows.

SANTANA Good mor'in, ma.

> [BB *rushes out after* MEBUDE. *He kicks the door shut with his heel. The party noises are immediately cut off.*]

Good mor'in, sah. I hope say di party de groovy?

BB Ebun!

MEBUDE I came out to be alone.

> [SANTANA *quietly slips back to his hut in the shadows.*]

BB Ebun. It's two o'clock in the morning.

MEBUDE Go back to them ...

BB Ebun.

MEBUDE Stop shouting my name at this hour of the night!

BB You'll come back in with me this very minute.

MEBUDE Go back to your mob.

[*The door swings open and* YINKA *lurches out, obviously several glasses up the road.*]

SANTANA [*from his hut, to* YINKA] Good mor'in, sah.

YINKA [*in an affected American accent*] Wuzzup, BB ma man?

BB [*to* YINKA, *a trifle impatiently*] Go back inside and leave us alone.

[YINKA *stops.*]

YINKA Did you say ...?

BB I said, leave us alone, Yinka.

YINKA That's what you said?

BB That's what I said. I said ...

YINKA You're asking me to leave you alone?

BB [*heatedly*] That's what I ...

YINKA Is that how you talk to a brother? [*to* MEBUDE] Is that how he talks to a brother?

[MEBUDE *pointedly ignores him.*]

BB We're having a very private conversation here, Yinka.

YINKA 'A very private conversation.' [*to* MEBUDE] You heard him. He's calling me a stranger. I who walked through broken glass with him. I who stepped on nails and burning rocks, courted bullets and taunted death with him, not once, not twice, but more times than I can remember, and what does he say to me? 'We are having a very private conversation.' [*Reflective pause. Then, decidedly*] Hey, I'm a poet. That was sheer poetry.

BB You're drunk, Yinkus.

YINKA That's for you to say and ...[*burps*] ... me to decide.

BB Do me a favour, tell them in there to listen out for the phone. With the noise in there ...

YINKA Your father.

ACT ONE

[YINKA *heads back inside.*]

BB Yinkus...

YINKA Your grandfather.

BB Don't forget to keep an ear open for the phone.

[YINKA *disappears inside.*]

I love that clown.

[*Pause.*]

MEBUDE [*portentously*] What's this call you're expecting?

BB A very important one. It's been long in coming but worth the wait.

[MEBUDE *looks at him suspiciously.*]

[*dreamily*] I love Ketu. I love this land. [*waves widely around him*] I'm bound to it— by blood. I was born right here on this spot, did I ever tell you that? My mother, before she died, she said to me, made me promise... She said to me, Bikan—she never called me BB—she said Bikan, always remember your roots. Always. [*gestures towards the house*] That's why I built that here. I brought down the old mud thing and built that in its place. People say to me, BB, why do you live in this land of hovels, in the midst of these—these shanties, this poverty? Why don't you move to Ikoyi, or Victoria Island, somewhere more befitting your class and status? I say to them—

MEBUDE [*on cue*] I'm bound to it by blood. Yes. Yes. But what's all this got to do with my question?

BB This is my—kingdom. I walk the streets and people follow me. They come to me with their problems small and big. And I—I try my best. My best.

MEBUDE You made me a promise, BB.

BB A promise?

MEBUDE A promise.

BB I'm a man of my word, yes.

MEBUDE You made me a promise, BB.

BB I did? Then I'm sure I kept it. Whatever it is, I'm sure I kept it.

MEBUDE You said, never again.

BB Never—did I? Never again what? Haji Santa!

SANTANA [*off*] Sah.

[SANTANA *hurries out from his shed.*]

MEBUDE Leave the man alone, BB.

SANTANA [*to* MEBUDE] Mesef?

BB Haji Santa.

SANTANA God bless you, sah.

BB How long have I known you?

SANTANA Mesef, sah?

BB How long have you worked here?

SANTANA Sorry, sah. Two years, sah.

BB Where did we first meet?

MEBUDE On a garbage dump under Eko bridge.

BB Where, Haji Santa, did I first set eyes on you?

SANTANA [*puzzled*] Sah?

BB Where did I first set eyes on you?

SANTANA But Madam have said it, sah.

BB [*patiently*] I know Madam have said it.

SANTANA I beg your padding, sah. Na for under Eko bridge, God bless you, sah.

BB And what state were you in?

SANTANA Lagos State, sah.

[MEBUDE *sniggers.*]

I beg your padding, sah. Na bad condition I been de, bad bad condition.

BB [*to* MEBUDE] It was raining that evening. Around

this time of night. My car had broken down under the bridge. Of all places. I got out to check the engine. Haji Santa was huddled by the foot of the bridge, in a blanket, wet. He helped push the car. We got it started.

SANTANA True talk, sah, true talk.

BB As a token of my appreciation...

MEBUDE You offered him money. Which he wouldn't accept.

BB I offered him money, which he wouldn't accept...

MEBUDE You were impressed.

BB I was impressed.

> [*Pause.*]

> I was impressed. I said to him, young man, what can I do for you?

SANTANA True talk, sah, true talk.

BB He said, find me a job. Get me out of this dump. I gave him my card and said, drop by tomorrow. I promised to get him a job.

> [*He pauses to check his watch and glances in the direction of the house.*]

> He came the next day, at the appointed hour, and I got him a job. Better still, I gave him a job. I made him a watchman. I gave him pride in himself. [*to* MEBUDE] I promise— I deliver.

> [*He dismisses* SANTANA *with a wave.*]

MEBUDE Why is Yinka here tonight? And those other ones in there?

BB [*patiently*] Because we are having a party here tonight, perhaps?

MEBUDE Rubbish, BB. Give me some credit for knowing you better than that. You're up to something. And whatever it is, I don't want to have a hand in it.

You hear me? I don't want to have a hand in it.

[*Pause.*]

I need to think of the future.

[BB *goes to the door. He listens, then returns.*]

BB   The future is now.

MEBUDE   This is all a joke to you, not so? Not so? [*Pause.*] You wouldn't be here, here tonight, celebrating, if it wasn't for me, Bikan Babarinsa. You'd be six foot under the earth, riddled with bullets and in some mass grave God-knows-where. [*Pause.*] If it hadn't been for my father...

BB   I know.

MEBUDE   If...

BB   I know.

MEBUDE   I went crying to him.

BB   Baby, baby, baby.

MEBUDE   I said—don't baby, baby me—I said if you let them shoot BB, if you let them so much as touch a hair on him, I'm...

BB   You saved my life, yes, yes.

MEBUDE   And this for someone who loathes your type with every breath in his body.

BB   I'm...

MEBUDE   People like you, creeps like you...

BB   ...not a type.

MEBUDE   He couldn't understand how I could come asking him to save the neck of someone like you, he wanted to know why, to understand...

BB   To understand.

MEBUDE   He wanted to understand. I said to him: love.

BB   Love?

MEBUDE   That's what he said. *Love?* He called my mum.

ACT ONE

Come hear your daughter, he said to her, she is lecturing me about love. We send a child to college, to get a degree, just so she can come and tell us that she's in *love* with scum?

BB Scum? That's me? That's what I am?

MEBUDE He saved your life.

BB He did, didn't he? Never underestimate the kindness of strangers. [*Pause.*] The fact that I was in a position to line a few pockets came in handy as well though.

MEBUDE [*patiently*] It wouldn't have mattered how much you could spend...

BB No?

MEBUDE No. The knives were out for you.

BB They were?

MEBUDE A whole suitcase of commodities, remember? That's what they found in the house. A whole suitcase.

BB A whole suitcase.

MEBUDE Punishable by death by firing squad.

BB I know, I know. My lawyers...

MEBUDE Yes. What could your lawyers have done?

BB My lawyers...

MEBUDE Yes?

BB ...could've done sweetall, I admit, without the generous assistance of your good father, and I shall always be in his debt.

MEBUDE I don't like the tone of your voice, BB.

BB Which one you de now? What's happened to your sense of humour?

[YINKA *appears by the doorway.*]

YINKA Lissen, you two, I know say nothing concern me for this palaver-o, but, man, I have to tell you that you're being fucking rude to your guests. That's all I have to say. [*to* BB] Your call's come through.

[YINKA *goes back inside.*]

BB [*preparing to go*] Are you coming inside then?

MEBUDE It was my birthday tonight, BB.

BB That's hardly a state secret.

MEBUDE If you were going to get your old 'friends' together to plan something that will undoubtedly land you in front of a firing squad, it shouldn't have been tonight.

BB I don't know about you but I don't like these mosquitos.

MEBUDE You promised.

BB [*turning to go into the house*] Woman, get a life, will you?

MEBUDE BB.

[*He stops.*]

BB Yes?

[*She flings a shoe at him.*]

Scene Two

A moment later.

ADAMA *comes out of the house, dragging with her a drunken* MAN. ADAMA *tugs at* BB's *sleeve as he makes to go past her.*

ADAMA [*to* BB] Just a minute!

[MEBUDE *goes into the house. She makes a point of ignoring* ADAMA *as she leaves. The* MAN *sidles into a corner.*]

BB Ada, there's someone on the phone for me.

ACT ONE

ADAMA Just thirty seconds, BB. We've got to be off in another minute. Beside, I'd been waiting all evening for a private moment with you, and then you disappeared with your woman.

   [*The* MAN *retches.*]

BB Looks like you're in for a very romantic time tonight.

ADAMA He'll be fine. [*to the* MAN] Are you alright, darling?

   [*The* MAN *retches in response.*]

   He'll be alright. It's that combination of scotch and palm wine. Sometimes it can be a killer.

BB Who's he?

ADAMA Michael Jackson. [*pulls* BB *aside*] I'm worried, BB. About you.

BB That's what I pay you to do, Ada. Worry about me.

ADAMA There're stories going round, BB. Your name's being mentioned in circumstances that make me uneasy.

BB What exactly have you heard?

ADAMA Come on!

BB Your sources are pathetically off the mark. As always.

ADAMA There are limits to the miracles even I can conjure. We only escaped last time by the skin of our teeth. If it hadn't been for your woman's father...

BB Stop referring to her as 'my woman'. She has a name, and it isn't 'my woman'.

ADAMA And you know their condition for letting you go...

BB A hundred grand to the judge, half a million to the military tribunal, two fifty grand to...

ADAMA You are mistaking the cost of obtaining with the condition itself. In case you forgot—which I'm certain you haven't—they let you go only on condition that you stayed away permanently from dealing in what you call commodities.

BB And I have too, Ada. That was a year ago. I haven't dealt in 'that' since.

[ADAMA *makes an impatient gesture.*]

ADAMA The government is very, very sensitive at the moment. The vice-president was summoned last week for a serious discussion with the American ambassador. An alarming number of our compatriots are being apprehended all over the world. Mules. The Americans are asking the government to do something about it or else...

BB Spare me the details.

YINKA [*off*] Where are you, BB? It's fucking long-distance, you know!

BB One second, Yinkus. [*to* ADAMA] I'm just a businessman. You are the lawyer. 'Michael Jackson'. You and your toy-boys.

[BB *hurries inside, shaking his head in amusement.* ADAMA *goes to the* MAN.]

ADAMA Are you alright?

[*The* MAN *vomits on her. She stands, looking at him with a mixture of pity and disgust at him and at herself.*]

Scene Three

A moment later.

MEBUDE *is alone. She rummages through her bag and finds a rumpled pack of cigarettes. She searches in vain for a light. She slaps out at mosquitos.*

YINKA *comes out. He offers her a light.*

YINKA Something strange happened to me last week.

MEBUDE Something strange is always happening to you, Yinka.

YINKA I was at Falomo shopping centre. Shopping.

MEBUDE That *is* strange. Where was the errand girl?

[YINKA *looks at her, not comprehending.*]

That one you call your wife.

YINKA [*ignoring her remark*] As I made for a checkout counter I heard from behind me a voice. Someone calling out my name. I turned round and...

MEBUDE And?

YINKA I turn round and this old guy comes running. Are you Yinka? he says. I look him up and down. I was sure I'd never seen him before. He mentions my parents' names. So I say yes, I was. Yinka. He punched the air for joy. Don't you tell me you don't recognise me, because that's when I'll really be upset, he said. Well, I didn't know him from Thunder Balogun and I said so. Did you grow up in Ketu? he asked me. I did. He even knew the precise address. He'd lived next door to us some twenty-five years back, he said. I was still unable to place his face. His next question cleared any doubts I might have had. Did you, at the time, own a big black dog called Bingo? Yes, I said. Killed in a hit-and-run. Bingo's neck was broken, wasn't it? Snapped around here. He gestured mysteriously towards his own neck. I strained forward to see whatever it was he was trying to show me. Go on, he said, touch my neck.

[YINKA *pulls* MEBUDE's *hand over his neck. Then he issues a savage 'woof'.* MEBUDE *jumps.* YINKA *is in stitches.*]

Just thought that'd cheer you up!

MEBUDE Oh really?

YINKA [*seriously*] He does that to you all the time, doesn't he, play pranks on you?

MEBUDE Who?

YINKA BB. Who else? I think it's—sickening.

MEBUDE You do?

YINKA Jokes aside, honestly. You women. Why is it always the guy who, the only words he knows are 'wham, bam, thank you', why is it always he who wins your heart?

MEBUDE Is that an informed opinion?

YINKA I'm not joking.

MEBUDE By God, it's true! You're not.

YINKA Go on, laugh at me. All I'm saying is—and Lord knows I love that sonofabitch like a brother—all I'm saying is, that guy has no regard for you, no respect whatsoever. Go in there right this very moment, he's trying to score with one of the singers.

MEBUDE Why are you telling me all this?

YINKA You know why.

MEBUDE He'll kill you.

YINKA What makes you think he doesn't know? He simply doesn't give a damn. Tell me, what's he got that no-one else's got?

MEBUDE How about, I like him?

YINKA That's all?

MEBUDE That's all.

YINKA Has he— what...what is it, what is it you see in him? Talk to me, sister: what are you after? His money?

MEBUDE [*half amused, half irritated*] What do you think?

YINKA What do I think?

MEBUDE What do you think?

YINKA No, I suppose it wouldn't be for the money, not for a woman like you, someone of your background.

MEBUDE [*sarcastically*] No?

YINKA Lucky bastards. Guys like your father. They had it the easy way, is what I say. All that oil money to steal from. [*Reflective pause.*] Lucky bastards.

MEBUDE My father might have been guilty of a great many things, including being an insufferable tyrant, a double-faced bastard as well as being a judge, but stealing oil money simply wasn't one of his vocations.

YINKA I said guys like him... You know why guys like me and BB, why guys like us went into commodities?

MEBUDE Good old-fashioned greed?

YINKA Pure business acumen. We identified a niche in the market, a classic situation where demand far exceeded supply, and we went for it.

MEBUDE You haven't done too badly, considering.

YINKA At a price, though. At a price. But—no, not bad at all. I have everything I ever wanted in life. Everything. And I've gone totally legit. No more shady deals for me. Only the occasional heist these days, nothing too risky, and only for old times' sakes. You know: chop and clean mouth like say nothing happen... [*demonstrates by wiping his mouth with an imaginary handkerchief*] Only thing that's lacking is—and I swear to God, the only one thing that's lacking in my life is—a decent woman.

[MEBUDE *is roaring with laughter by now.*]

Laugh all you want. As long as you remember

	you'll never get your way with BB. He simply isn't the marrying type.
MEBUDE	Says who?
YINKA	You'd better believe me. On the other hand, if you're looking for the marrying kind...
MEBUDE	He's standing here in front of me, right?
YINKA	We're thinking with one mind. We'll make the ideal couple.
MEBUDE	Trio. How's that wife of yours?
YINKA	Alive, and fine, and not complaining, thank you. You know what I like about you? Obviously, your beauty... But you know what I really like?
MEBUDE	What?
YINKA	Your intelligence.
MEBUDE	Really. Tell me about it.
YINKA	You like books, don't you? I do too.
MEBUDE	I do too too.
YINKA	What?
MEBUDE	Joke.

[YINKA *pauses briefly to reflect over the joke. He quickly gives up.*]

YINKA I like books, you see, only I don't have time to read the damn things. Literature was my favourite subject at school. 'Friends, Romans, Countrymen, lend me your ears, I come to bury Caesar, not to praise him.' Who said that?

MEBUDE Oh, fuck off, Yinka.

YINKA No, really, really, really, who said that? And to whom? On what occasion?

MEBUDE Brutus...?

YINKA Wrong, wrong, wrong. Answer: a man in a brothel trying to make out with a good-time woman holding his dick in admiration!

[BB *comes out. He is in a jubilant mood.*]

BB   I'm coming out of retirement.

[YINKA *stops laughing.*]

YINKA   I wasn't aware you were retired in the first place.

BB   Commodities.

MEBUDE   You're *what*?

BB   I've been working on this for almost a year. I've promised myself it's going to be my last.

MEBUDE   And it involves commodities?

BB   [*to* YINKA] She wants to know if it involves commodities. Tell her, tell the woman.

YINKA   [*to* BB] Tell her what? [*to* MEBUDE] What do you think this is—Sesame Street?

MEBUDE   Keep out of this, Yinka, just stay well clear of this. You weren't here last year when we were running around trying to save BB's neck.

YINKA   [*to* BB] She's telling me to keep out of this.

MEBUDE   Go back to Europe.

YINKA   [*to* BB] She's telling me to go back to Europe.

MEBUDE   Those drug squad people chasing you all over Europe will welcome you with very open arms. [*to* BB] It's occurred to you of course that you'll effectively be breaking your probation and that this time, if anything goes wrong, my dad might not be so willing to intervene?

BB   Stuff your dad. And stop speaking to me like I'm out to lunch or something

YINKA   [*to* BB, *tentatively*] Baba BB ...

BB   Yes?

YINKA   This—caper?

BB   Yes? What 'caper'? [*laughing*] 'Caper', 'caper' ... Yinkus-the-Yankee!

YINKA [*à la Robert de Niro*] You talkin' to me? You talkin' to me? [*'looks' behind him*] Then who the hell else are you talkin' to? You talkin' to me? Well I am the only one here... who the fuck d'you think you're talkin' to?

[*He draws an imaginary gun.*]

BB [*ducking*] Americana-Yinkus!

YINKA [*à la Marlon Brando, drawing*] I'm a superstitious man.

BB [*ducking*] Americana-Yinkus!

YINKA [*shooting*] The dead stay dumb.

BB [*ducking and drawing*] Yinkus-the-Yinkus!

YINKA You're dead without money.

BB Yinkus-Yinkus!

YINKA That's the way the cookie crumbles.

[*They 'shoot out' simultaneously and both 'die'.*]

MEBUDE Since you two boys seem to be getting on so fine, I think I'll just leave you alone for a moment.

[*She makes to leave.*]

BB Excuse me? What did you call us just then?

MEBUDE You were having so much fun with your nostalgia-without-memory game, I thought I should leave you to it.

BB You called us children.

MEBUDE You were behaving like children.

BB You called me a child.

MEBUDE I'm waiting for you to let go of my arm.

YINKA 'Nostalgia-without-memory.' Write that down, Santana. I wish God had given me the brains to coin phrases like that. It's so... so you, Ebun. Congratulations on a first-class brain.

BB [*to* MEBUDE, *with unexpected vehemence*] You Daddy's pet.

YINKA I could've said that.

BB What?

YINKA Daddy's pet. I'm sorry, BB, but that's still no match for 'nostalgia-without-memory'. To come up with anything close to that you'll need a brand-new brain on that neck of yours.

BB Why don't you learn to shut up just for once, Yinka? How come you have a mouth like a conveyer-belt?

YINKA [*moving away*] Hey, hey, I'm not the one who just called you a child.

[BB *is holding* MEBUDE *in a firm grip.*]

BB [*to* YINKA] Are you in?

YINKA Am I in on what? Wait a minute, BB, I think I've slightly lost track.

BB Are you in or not?

YINKA You don't understand, BB, I only came here tonight for the party. You didn't warn me in advance. You should've warned me in advance.

[*A loud noise from the direction of* SANTANA's *shed stops them all in their tracks. There are sounds of a minor skirmish.* SANTANA *appears at the fringes of the light, his hands raised in the air. He is followed immediately by* INSPECTOR KAMORU, *who has commandeered* SANTANA's *rifle and is now digging it into his back and prodding him forward with it.*]

KAMORU Good morning, Baba BB.

BB Inspector Kamoru!

[YINKA *whistles in relief.* BB *does not betray his emotions.* MEBUDE *wears a tense, wary look.*]

KAMORU I must say I'm rather surprised, BB. A man in

	your line of job... What happened to your bodyguards? I could've been anybody, you know, anybody.
YINKA	Morning, Inspector.
SANTANA	Terribly sorry, sah. He catch me by surprise.
BB	I've no need for bodyguards, Inspector.
KAMORU	Come on, BB. Where's the retinue of bodyguards you used to have round the clock?
BB	Age has made me a wiser man, Inspector. The day I wake up and find that I need protection from my own people, then... (I'm fucked.)
KAMORU	In my experience, all the animals come out at night.
BB	Yes. [*to* SANTANA] Santana?
SANTANA	Sah? Beg your padding, sah.

[SANTANA *leaves.*]

BB [*to* KAMORU *with a wry smile*] I'm sure you haven't come here at this hour to lecture me on the wisdom of self-protection, Inspector.

KAMORU No, you're right. I haven't. [*to* MEBUDE] I was with your father the other evening, at his place. [*pointedly*] We were hoping to see you there. It was your brother's anniversary. Two years since he left us for the great beyond.

MEBUDE I was there in spirit, Uncle Kamoru.

KAMORU We played his favourite music, depleted your father's brandy collection and chattered through the night.

MEBUDE Good evening, Uncle Kamoru.

[MEBUDE *heads back into the house.* YINKA *follows her.*]

KAMORU [*to* MEBUDE] I hope that one of these days you'll find time to go and visit him. He is still your father.

ACT ONE

BB   I didn't know you were related.

KAMORU   There are many things you don't know, BB. I carried that woman in my arms when she was a child, you know.

BB   We've both got something in common then.

KAMORU   Have we?

BB   We've both carried her in our arms. [*laughs*] Laugh, Inspector. That was funny.

KAMORU   Was it?

BB   Yes, Inspector.

> [*He tickles* KAMORU. KAMORU *laughs, protesting. Pause.*]

KAMORU   My apologies for barging in in this manner. I was passing by in my patrol car when I happened to look this way— and, well, you were outside, the lights were on, and I could hear music... Beside, there was something I'd been meaning to come over and discuss with you.

BB   You couldn't have stopped by at a better time, Inspector. It so happens that it's Ebun's birthday and we are having a party.

KAMORU   It's Ebun's birthday, eh? Very like me to forget these things. Only the other day I was standing with my wife at the supermarket and I suddenly realised that I'd completely forgotten her name. Can you believe that? And to think we've been married thirty years now. I mean, we've been together that long. Mind you, she had a dream last night and didn't recognise me.

BB   She told you that?

KAMORU   She didn't need to tell me. I was in the dream.

BB   Of course, Inspector. Would you like to step inside for a moment, have a beer?

KAMORU   You're too kind, BB. I'd really like to do that, but as it happens, I'm on duty tonight. [*Pause.*] I shall be very brief, BB. The situation is this: a little under a year ago, a consignment of substances now believed to be—commodities—worth several million dollars at street value was intercepted at the International airport. It was found in luggage belonging to a well-known Lagos socialite. She was arrested and held for questioning prior to laboratory analyses of the impounded substances.

BB I don't see how this concerns me, Inspector, or how I can be of any help.

KAMORU Please, BB... A few hours after the arrest, some burglars broke into our central forensic laboratories. They made away, not only with the impounded substances, but with several other 'exhibits' from other cases pending. In the end the suspect had to be released for lack of evidence. As you know, since the press had their usual field day bashing the Force for weeks afterwards, it was a serious dent on our reputation...

BB [*laughing*] I'm learning that for the first time.

KAMORU What?

BB That you had a reputation, let alone a dented one.

> [KAMORU *joins in the laughter even though it's obvious he hasn't found the joke entirely rib-cracking.*]

KAMORU Ah! You are such a funny person... We put word out on the street.

BB I still fail to see how this concerns me.

KAMORU Patience, now. Na softly softly we de catch monkey. We heard nothing for almost a year. No word at all. Then a few days ago... a few days ago we had our first break. Word came to us about the movement of an unusually high amount of 'commodities' on the streets. We knew we were back on the trail of the missing 'substances'. But just as we thought we were on the verge of cracking it, the investigation came up against a brick wall. Just like that. *Fiam!* Our source went silent. On account he was ambushed one night by person or persons unknown, and his throat neatly slit open.

[*Pause.*]

BB   Naturally, he became silent?

KAMORU   Your name was mentioned.

BB   My name was mentioned.

KAMORU   Yes, BB. In connection with this—whole affair.

BB   [*amiably*] That's a slur on my reputation, Inspector.

KAMORU   You misunderstand me. I've come for help. Not to slander you. I know you for... [*tongue-in-cheek*]... an abiding pillar of the community. A generous man.

BB   Do you still keep that rather nice little BMW you won on the lottery?

KAMORU   [*momentarily lost*] On the lottery? Oh, yes, the lottery! No, had to sell it, I'm afraid. Times are hard, BB. One of my boys, you see, won a scholarship to England. To study engineering. I had to sell the car to raise the flight tickets.

BB   [*in admiration*] If I'd had a father like you, I'd be a different person today.

KAMORU   If I'd had a son like you, BB, I'd be serving a murder sentence.

[*They both laugh.* KAMORU *looks around as if to make sure they are alone.*]

If anyone sees me here, I'm finished. I just thought I owed this to you: to warn you.

[BB *begins to protest his innocence.*]

No, no, I believe you. I thought I should warn you. The heat is on. The new military boys are very touchy about it all.

BB   I hear you. I hear you loud and clear.

KAMORU   That's all I ask of you, just this one favour: if you could keep your ear close to the ground, as they say, and if anything crops up...

BB   Say no more, Inspector. If anything crops up—the slightest whisper—and you can trust that I'll be on the phone to you. Now, Inspector, that dealt with, I insist you come inside for a drink.

KAMORU   I'm afraid...

BB   I insist.

[*He leads the* INSPECTOR *inside.*]

Scene Four

A moment later. A wizened OLD MAN *comes on riding a bicycle.* SANTANA *comes out of his hut as the* OLD MAN *is dismounting.*

SANTANA   Which kind stupidness be dis? Dis place look like parking space for your eye?

[*The* OLD MAN *turns and* SANTANA *beams in recognition.*]

Grandpa! It's you, Grandpa.

[*He rushes up to him and prostrates himself in greeting.*]

Grandpa, how are you? Why didn't you warn me in advance that you were coming? Do you know what time it is? This town is no longer as safe as it used to be, you know.

ACT ONE

OLD MAN I encountered some men
of the night on the way, men in hoods,
waylaying cars with their sawn-off guns.
They paused for a while when I passed them by,
throwing greetings and wishing me well.
Even they still give some due to age.
Your grandmother sends her blessings and her love.

SANTANA It's been five years or more, Grandpa.

OLD MAN I have lain still for so long now,
it's always a treat to come out
and stretch the feet.
Don't bother to get me a seat.

SANTANA It's so good to see you, Grandpa. Is father well? Have you seen mother? Did you stop by at the village?

OLD MAN I called on them yesterday.
Your father had only complaints. As usual.
I broke a colanut and threw in a proverb,
and he stopped baying at once.

SANTANA Well, Grandpa, this is where I work.

OLD MAN It's not a prince's job,
I can see that at once.
But I smell your sweat everywhere
so you must be doing some good.

SANTANA You must meet my boss. He's a tough nut but a really nice man.

OLD MAN Even lunatics
have their moments of peace.
But you still chant a prayer
when they knock on your door.

SANTANA I do not understand your words.

OLD MAN You do not test the depth
of a river with both feet, my son.

OLD MAN   This house is a raging stream.
          It will sweep away both the fisherman
          and his haul.

SANTANA   You lose me even further. I do not understand you at all.

OLD MAN   You have been here long enough.
          You have been in this den
          of thieves for quite a while.
          Now you must move on
          before they call you brother.

SANTANA   I'm only a gateman, Grandpa, not a thief in the night. I have lived by your words all the time. I'm not about to change.

OLD MAN   The witness of a rat
          is himself another rat.
          Pack your bag and leave.

SANTANA   I have no place to go if I leave. They gave me shelter here when I slept in ditches. They took pity on me when the world turned its back on me.

OLD MAN   God will sometimes
          have his little jokes.
          You must always allow for that.
          Pack your bags and leave this place.

SANTANA   And go where, Grandpa? Back to the rodents and roaches beneath the bridge? Back to those streets where 'honest' people spat on me? Leave me alone, Grandpa. Go away. I'll shut my eyes. When I open them you'll have disappeared.

OLD MAN   I've had my say.
          I shall go now.

SANTANA   If I must leave, you have to tell me where to go.

OLD MAN   How old are you now?

SANTANA   You know how old I am.

OLD MAN   Yes, but you must damn yourself
          with your own lips.

ACT ONE

SANTANA Twenty last year.

OLD MAN When we find a bride for a man,
we do not also consummate the marriage for him.
Wait another twenty years.
Perhaps you'll understand my words.

SANTANA I understand your words. But I want to be rich too, Grandpa. Like them. I want to ride in a car and build a house in Maroko.

OLD MAN You are still a child.
Look up there.
What do you see?

SANTANA The sky. The moon and stars.

OLD MAN Observe that moon carefully,
you might learn a thing or two.
It moves slowly but it crosses the town.

> [*He swings his bicycle round and begins to leave.*]

SANTANA Goodnight, Grandpa. Will I see you again?

OLD MAN Every day. Wherever you may be.

> [*He leaves.*]

SANTANA Say me well to Grandma.

> [MEBUDE *comes out.*]

MEBUDE Who was that? Were you talking to someone?

SANTANA My grandfather. Came to have a word.

MEBUDE At this hour? Where does he live?

SANTANA Mushin Cemetery.

MEBUDE Why didn't you get him a cab?

SANTANA He doesn't need one.

MEBUDE Did you say...?

SANTANA Yes. Mushin Cemetery. He's been there now well over twelve years.

MEBUDE Your grandfather lives in a cemetery?

SANTANA They had to bury him someplace.

MEBUDE Don't get smart with me, and stop talking nonsense. How can your grandfather visit you if he's been dead and buried twelve years?

SANTANA I don't know. I'll ask him next time I see him.

MEBUDE Are you on drugs or something? [*Pause.*] Must be your own tepid brand of humour.

SANTANA I tell you say no be joke, Madam Ebun. That was my grandfather. I was eight when he died. He visits—now and again.

MEBUDE Na only you know. That's not why I came out. Okay, you can bring it out now.

SANTANA Madam Ebun...

MEBUDE Stop fretting. They're all drunk out of their senses in there. I don't think they're in any hurry to come out.

> [SANTANA *reaches for a package in the shed and hands it over to her.*]

SANTANA Happy birthday!

MEBUDE [*unwrapping the package*] I still remember my tenth birthday. Mother was still alive, and father...he had high hopes for me. He didn't think Dele, my brother, had enough brains between his ears to cross a street without getting knocked down by a bicycle. But me, he simply worshipped. He was going to make a lawyer of me.

> [SANTANA *helps her to open the package.*]

SANTANA What happened on your tenth birthday, Madam Ebun?

MEBUDE I wanted to become an Iroko tree.

> [SANTANA *looks on with slightly exaggerated interest.*]

I'd just been on a trip to my mother's parents in

the village. While there my grandfather had taken me to see his farm. He showed me an Iroko tree. Told me about its powers, about the spirits that lived in it. About the people who go to it from all over to offer sacrifice and to ask favours of it: the barren, the blind, the poor, the rich. And he said, what's more, it always made a dream come true. 'We all need an Iroko tree in our lives sometimes', he said. I was enchanted. I told him I wanted to be an Iroko tree. He told me it was the easiest thing in the world. I took it literally, and made up my mind that what I wanted for my next birthday was to be transformed into an Iroko tree. And so when my tenth came along, and it didn't happen, I cried all day long.

[*She has now finished unwrapping the package.*]

Uuumh. A necklace. It's—nice.

[*She tries it on, swinging round so he can help knot it up. She turns again and faces him.*]

Well, thank you. I brought you some whisky.

SANTANA [*proudly, almost shyly*] I make am myself.

[MEBUDE *runs her hands over the necklace.*]

MEBUDE It's beautiful. [*Pause.*] You are beautiful. Come here. Hold me.

[SANTANA *looks around in alarm.*]

SANTANA Madam Ebun...

MEBUDE Come on. Hold me.

SANTANA Madam.

[MEBUDE *puts a finger across his lips.*]

MEBUDE Sssh. I said hold me.

[SANTANA *holds her. She caresses his crotch.* YINKA *comes out and watches them with disbelief.*]

MEBUDE What are you staring at? Haven't you ever seen a man and a woman together?

>[*As* YINKA *makes to respond, a middle-aged man appears from the direction of* SANTANA's *hut. He is* ETE KAMBA BASSEY. *Silence as the others turn to look at him.* MEBUDE *lets go of* SANTANA *awkwardly.*]

Father.

>[BASSEY *stands looking first at* MEBUDE, *then at the others, not saying a thing. Then he turns round as suddenly as he had appeared and goes away, a sad, lost look on his face. They watch him leave in silence.*]

YINKA God, I hate these mosquitos.

>[*He turns and heads back inside.*]

End of Act One

Act Two

GOD SAVE THE KING

Scene One

A few weeks later. Early morning, just before the working day begins.

A courthouse in Lagos.

Chief Justice ETE KAMBA BASSEY's *private chambers.* BASSEY's *desk is bare. Aside from a portable tape recorder and the telephone, the only item on it is a framed photograph of a young man.*

BASSEY *is on the telephone. In front of him is* ADAMA *and, by the door,* SANTANA, *standing diffidently. He genuflects almost every time* BASSEY *glances in his direction.*

BASSEY [*on the phone*] Yes, hello? [*shifts heavily in his robes*] Is that— you, idiot boy? Is that you, Akunakuna? [*to* ADAMA] My houseboy: he has an intellect the size of a mosquito's egg and the proficiency of a lawnmower... [*makes to mouth something into the phone*] ...that's broken down. [*on the phone*] Akunakuna? *Akunakuna?* [*to* ADAMA] All he ever does is, yetcha, yetcha. [*mouths something into the phone*] As you might have guessed, I wasn't the one who hired him. Blame that on the wife. [*on the phone*] Akunakuna, is Madam...? [*Pause. Finally:*] No. Did she say—? She didn't? At... [*checks the time*] ...eight in the morning? Are you sure she didn't? Positive? Okay.

> [*He hangs up. After a long silence, and to no-one in particular, he speaks again.*]

I think my wife is having an affair.

> [ADAMA *shifts uneasily.* SANTANA *makes what he perceives to be the obligatory fawning noises. He ceases this when* BASSEY *stops him with a long searching look.*]

Never mind. [*slips on a pair of reading glasses*] So, Madam, what can I do for you?

> [*He notices* SANTANA.]

I haven't had the pleasure of meeting the gentleman by the door, have I?

SANTANA You mean mesef, sah? Sorry, sah.

ADAMA [*to* SANTANA, *with irritation*] I told you to wait outside.

SANTANA Mesef? I been t'ink say Madam go need me for any messengering, ma.

ADAMA Mr Santana...

SANTANA Santa for chut, ma.

ADAMA What? Oh, yes, I see what you mean. No, I shan't be needing you for anything, but thanks for the offer. Could you go outside now and wait. Please. Santa?

> [SANTANA *dashes forward and prostrates himself before* BASSEY.]

SANTANA I take God and Orisha beg you oga mi sah, to be very merciful for my master, for even as di Good Book have said it, before John-the-Baptist Christ was, and cast your bread upon di waters for in my father's house there are many manchuns and whosoever comet to me shall not perich but have everlasting life.

> [ADAMA *stands up and leads the delirious* SANTANA *to the door.*]

After God sah, is you next to him!

[*He leaves.*]

BASSEY Who was that?

ADAMA [*apologetic and seething all at once*] An employee of my client's, your honour.

BASSEY Rather excitable fellow.

ADAMA I put it down to a deep sense of loyalty. And for good reason too. As I recall, he was literally picked up—by my client—from the streets of Lagos in a state of near starvation, whence he was restored to health, fed and clothed, and provided with a job.

BASSEY A Good Samaritan then he is, your—client?

ADAMA Absolutely. His Brother's Keeper. You've struck the nail on the head.

BASSEY A variation on the theme of Robin Hood, one might say?

ADAMA Literature is not my forte, your honour, so I shall confine myself to the Biblical allusion. A Good Samaritan. Very apt.

[*Pause.*]

Your honour...

BASSEY Ms Lawal?

ADAMA I know that out there in the courtroom yesterday and throughout the week we've been subjected to an unrelenting assault on my client's reputation, his character...

BASSEY A piece of advice, Ms Lawal?

ADAMA Your honour?

BASSEY Why don't you save all this for your summing-up?

ADAMA My summing-up...

BASSEY Just a thought.

[*Pause.*]

ADAMA A man in BB's position invariably attracts envy, enemies. You'll agree with me that one of the real tragedies of our society is this propensity of our people to find it easier to commiserate rather than rejoice, to condole rather than congratulate. The man who fails is welcomed with sympathetic noises. The man who succeeds is brought down so that he can become a recipient of sympathy.

BASSEY I do believe that a closing speech would be better served by such oratory, Ms Lawal.

ADAMA My client has enemies in high places, those who do not possess one speck of good in them and find it impossible to believe there are actually good people in the world, that there still exist people of integrity...

BASSEY Get to the point.

ADAMA Sorry?

BASSEY You have precisely two minutes to state your business and get out of my chambers.

ADAMA [*to the point*] I'm here to discuss a matter of—shall we say—premiums?

BASSEY Premiums?

ADAMA We want assurances.

BASSEY Who are 'we'?

ADAMA My client. Myself.

> [BASSEY *goes to a drinks cabinet and brings out a bottle of brandy and glasses. He pours two drinks.*]

BASSEY In other words you're attempting to subvert the course of justice.

ADAMA [*laughs*] Let's put it this way: the best miracles are those that have been carefully rehearsed beforehand.

ACT TWO

BASSEY You admit then that only a miracle could save Mr Babarinsa?

ADAMA It's impossible to say whether your honour is in earnest or merely joking.

BASSEY You're trying to offer me a bribe, not so?

ADAMA A gift, your lordship. A free gift: above board, nothing beyond the pale, nothing infra dig. A mere gift, not a bribe.

BASSEY [*feigned surprise*] But what have I done to deserve this—gift? Or, more pertinently perhaps, what must I do to deserve this—gift?

ADAMA You're playing games on me, Chief.

BASSEY Am I?

ADAMA You can hardly be described as a dilettante in this sort of thing, can you?

    [*Pause.*]

BASSEY Alright, Ms Lawal. I shall be frank with you. No point in pretending to be the Incorruptible Judge. You know me too well to be impressed by that.

ADAMA What is it then? Are your hands tied?

    [BASSEY *laughs a sad laugh.*]

BASSEY No, no, nothing like that. This isn't an 'orders from above' situation. It's merely personal.

    [*He picks up the framed photograph on his desk and hands it to* ADAMA.]

Dele. My son. With my late first wife. Dele died two years ago. He was twenty.

ADAMA I was at the funeral, Chief. I remember Dele. A swimming pool accident, wasn't it?

    [*Pause.*]

BASSEY We fibbed about that, about the cause of his death. I lied. Dele died from an overdose of—substances. He was what they call a crackhead.

ADAMA I see.

BASSEY You see the situation I'm in. Someone like your client, some animal like your client—possibly your client—was responsible for the death of my son.

[*He goes to the door and opens it for* ADAMA.]

Remind me, Ms Lawal, what is the maximum penalty for your client's offence?

ADAMA You're pulling my leg once more, my lord.

BASSEY There isn't a maximum penalty. There's only one penalty: death by firing squad.

[*He waves* ADAMA *out.*]

You can inform your client that I shall be there on Bar Beach on That Day. For a picnic. I shall see you in court, Ms Lawal.

[ADAMA *pauses at the door.*]

ADAMA Your honour?

BASSEY Ms Lawal?

ADAMA You wouldn't have any other reason aside from Dele?

BASSEY Enlighten me.

ADAMA It wouldn't be because of your daughter Ebun?

BASSEY I do not have a daughter.

ADAMA Your honour.

[BASSEY *picks up a broom and begins to sweep the floor.* ADAMA *jumps out of the way.*]

You've missed your vocation.

[*She leaves.* BASSEY *goes back to his desk, fixes himself another drink. Whilst he is preoccupied with this,* MEBUDE *walks in and takes a seat.*]

MEBUDE [*abruptly*] You wanted to see me?

[BASSEY *hastily puts down his drink.*]

BASSEY I ...

[*He thinks again and picks up his drink.*]
Yes, sit down.

MEBUDE I am sitting down.

BASSEY Well, yes... you... did come after all. I didn't think you would.

MEBUDE [*bitterly, but wittily*] I am an obedient daughter, father. You kicked me out. I left. You sent for me. Here I am.

BASSEY [*painfully*] I... didn't kick you out, Ebun. I simply asked you to stop seeing that... fellow.

[*Silence.*]

MEBUDE [*checking her watch*] Father, I'm here. Why did you send for me?

BASSEY For one moment, just then, when you came in... I thought—I swear to God—I thought it was your mother. You are the spitting image of your mother. [*Pause. He swallows hard.*] I... just wanted to see you. You know. Just... see you.

Scene Two

Midday, the same day. A remand room in the courthouse.

ADAMA [*to* BB] I've tried everything. Everything. I even went to his house the other night. Nearly lost my ankle to a Doberman. It was no use meeting him this morning either.

[MEBUDE *comes in.*]

MEBUDE [*to* ADAMA] Have they decided what they're doing to Yinka?

ADAMA Before this he was already a wanted man in Germany, France, Switzerland, Portugal, Italy, the UK...

[MEBUDE *nods impatiently.*]

MEBUDE Yes, yes... Are they handing him over to them?

ADAMA [*looking her straight in the eye*] I'm afraid so. The only reason that doesn't arise regarding BB is because, as you know, we... [*smiling grimly at* BB] ... have friends in high places.

BB Accomplices in high places, she means. They can afford to hand over Yinka—poor, poor Yinka—because he has nothing to say about them. I, on the other hand...

MEBUDE How come they haven't lifted a finger to help you then?

[ADAMA *picks up her briefcase preparatory to leaving.*]

ADAMA That's the question I shall be asking the General at lunch today.

[*A look of suspicion flickers across her features.*]

[*to* MEBUDE] Or do you know something we don't?

[MEBUDE *shrugs.*]

BB [*to* ADAMA] You're having lunch with the General?

ADAMA Don't look at me. I'm as surprised as you are. I've left over a dozen messages for him since the trial began, and not once did he bother to respond. Then just as I'm leaving home this morning, the phone rings. It's him, the General. Half twelve this afternoon, he says. At Eko Hotel. [*checks the time*] Actually I'd better make a move now.

BB Give my regards to his pot-belly.

ADAMA Not to mention his creeping hands. I'd better be off.

[*As she leaves, the* POLICE ESCORTS *appear at the door.* ADAMA *blocks their way.*]

As you can see, my client is having a private word with his fiancée.

[*The* POLICE ESCORTS *leave reluctantly, followed by* ADAMA.]

MEBUDE I don't trust her.

BB Why on earth not?

MEBUDE Never have. Never will. She's too—smooth.

BB Up till now she's done a brilliant job. [*Pause.*] I sometimes wonder about her myself. She's alright though. For the time being.

MEBUDE Do you really think she can swing it this time?

BB I don't see why not. This is ...

MEBUDE ... Nigeria, after all. Anything goes. [*Pause.*] I saw him this morning.

[BB *stiffens in anticipation but tries to play cool.*]

BB Who?

MEBUDE My dad.

BB Really?

MEBUDE He sent for me, actually. Wanted to make up, patch up our differences. He asked forgiveness. Can you believe that?

BB No.

MEBUDE He used to say: I've never had any cause to regret any action, or judgement, I've taken.

BB Until you came along.

MEBUDE I was his favourite child.

BB You lived an enchanted life.

MEBUDE I grew to hate it.

BB I would too.

MEBUDE Serious. You cannot imagine how boring it was.

BB You're right. I cannot.

MEBUDE   That's why I fell for you.

BB   You fell for me? You make it sound like a con trick.

MEBUDE   You've changed, though. You've changed almost beyond recognition.

BB   I've simply learnt to dance the dance of the times.

MEBUDE   You're not the man I fell in love with.

BB   Who was the man you fell in love with?

MEBUDE   He was, well, a nicer man, a more patient man, good-looking, a bit conceited, but not excessively so. Ambitious, but not obsessively so. A struggling businessman, determined to find his niche, but not to the extent of dabbling into crime.

BB   I do not dabble. I embrace wholeheartedly. I go the whole hog, I grab and never let go, I gate-crash and refuse to leave. I never dabble. Part-time pickpockets dabble. Occasional prostitutes dabble, amateur conmen dabble. People who are not focussed dabble. Fools dabble. Dabblers never make up their minds whether to cross the street or hang out in the middle of the road. Traffic runs over dabblers. Life is not for dabblers. Life abhors dabblers. Life demands nothing less than absolute obsession. I am not a dabbler.

[*Pause.*]

MEBUDE   He told me to tell you he's willing to help one last time.

BB   Judging from his words in the court this morning no-one could've guessed that in a million years.

MEBUDE   He's trying to make up with me.

BB   I see.

MEBUDE   He'd like to help. But ...

BB   There is a but.

ACT TWO

MEBUDE There is a but.

BB Call me smart. He wants something for himself this time?

MEBUDE No. But he's close to retirement.

BB Well, then...

MEBUDE However. His old network is still there. *Esprit de corps* and all that shit. He cannot swing it alone. There are people higher up. They'll need to be seen.

BB Bastards!

MEBUDE Who?

BB The whole lot of them. Fucking hypocrites.

MEBUDE The word is, they were not happy at the method you chose to carry out the operation. Filling an entire flight with people stuffed up with substances is not the sort of thing that earns you national medals.

BB I did not fill an entire flight with people stuffed up with substances. There were only five of them on that flight. And that was standard procedure. You work on the assumption that one or two or three apprehended would be simply the red herring that'd make it possible for the others to slip through. What I didn't know in this instance was that...

[*They hear a wailing from the distance.*]

YINKA [*off*] You must let me see him. I insist...

BB What I didn't know...

[*A desperate-looking* YINKA *enters. He is handcuffed and escorted by* INSPECTOR KAMORU.]

YINKA You must do something, BB! They're taking me to the airport, they're handing me over to Interpol!

KAMORU For the tenth time, Anfani, stop whimpering...

YINKA [*to* BB] You must do something. You must.

KAMORU You're becoming an absolute nuisance, Anfani...

YINKA [*to* BB] If they hand me over to those people I'm finished, I'll never come out alive.

KAMORU *Stop whimpering*, Anfani. Look at BB here. Is he tearing his hair out? Is he sobbing like a spoilt child?

BB You heard the Inspector, Yinka. Stop whimpering.

YINKA [*trembling*] I'm trying, I'm trying...

[BB *shakes him till he has calmed down a bit.*]

BB Yinka, I've got just one question for you.

YINKA Yes, BB, ma main man!

BB What is your father's name?

YINKA I'm sorry?

BB My own father's name—my surname—is Babarinsa. What is *your* father's name?

YINKA You know my father's name. [*incredulously*] Alright. Anfani. My father's name is Anfani.

[BB *guides him gently in the direction of the door.*]

BB You are Anfani. I am Babarinsa.

[*He stops by the door.*]

Let everyone bear their father's name. Please take him away, Inspector.

YINKA BB. Help me, help me...

[INSPECTOR KAMORU *leads* YINKA *off.*]

MEBUDE But...

BB There goes a dabbler.

MEBUDE Why?

BB His incompetence got us into this mess.

MEBUDE It did?

BB The courier who blew the whistle on all the others was one of his women. He'd bragged to her, boasted to her that she wouldn't be the only mule on that flight. He'd even shown her a list. The creep. My fault of course, bringing him in in the first instance.

MEBUDE With friends like you, BB...

BB Hey-hey-hey, what could I have done for him? You tell me.

MEBUDE You could've shown you cared.

BB I do, you know, I do. [*thoughtfully*] There was a time, a long time ago, when we were like brothers, me and Yinka. We were born right across the street from each other, did I ever tell you that? But that was a long time ago. We became business partners. In business there are no brothers, no sisters, no mothers, no fathers.

[*He turns to face* MEBUDE.]

Have you slept with him?

[MEBUDE *waves this away in irritation.*]

He told me he caught you once searching for something between Santana's legs.

MEBUDE And you believed him?

BB I didn't know whether to believe him or not.

[*Pause.*]

MEBUDE He saw me flirting with Santana, and nearly had a fit.

BB The problem with Yinka—and I've only now sussed it out—is that he isn't the man his mother was. Remind me to kill that boy Santana when this is all over.

MEBUDE I've been thinking, BB.

BB Yes?

MEBUDE I've decided to go back and finish my degree.

[BB's *smile is faltering.*]

BB Yes?

MEBUDE After this is all over. [*Pause.*] I don't think we're good for each other.

BB You don't?

MEBUDE I don't, BB. I don't think you'll ever change. And I think I was mad to have ever thought I could make you change. This is your life. It's the only life you've ever known. And it's not the life I want to live.

BB I understand. I understand.

[*He doesn't.*]

[*quietly, reflectively*] When I was a child, I learnt to speak. I didn't learn to listen. I should have learnt to listen. [*Pause.*] I'm sorry, Ebun.

[*They hold each other. A noise from nearby reaches them.*]

MEBUDE What's that?

[INSPECTOR KAMORU *enters.*]

KAMORU [*apologetic*] I know we are making quite a racket out there. My apologies for the noise.

MEBUDE But what is it, Uncle Kamoru? What noise is that?

KAMORU Just a routine softening-up job, that's all. A rude detainee being dealt with by the boys.

MEBUDE Someone's being flogged?

[*The noise of the flogging is incessant.*]

KAMORU I'm afraid so, Ebun. [*to* BB] Your whimpering friend, actually. Spitting at an officer.

BB If anything happens to him as a result of this beating—

KAMORU He's in expert hands, rest assured.

BB —I shall hold you personally responsible. [*listens*] He's not even screaming.

KAMORU He's in expert hands.

MEBUDE [*to* KAMORU] You've got a gag over his mouth, is that it? Is that what you've done?

KAMORU We haven't put a gag over his mouth. It just happens that he's also having a meal this very moment.

BB He's being flogged, and he's having a meal?

KAMORU A loaf of wheatbread. Stuffed into his mouth. I suspect though that he must be having trouble chewing it.

[*The noise of flogging reaches fever pitch.*]

[*to* BB] Have you got a hunters' dance where you come from? In my village—[*to* MEBUDE] yours too—we have a hunters' dance. It goes something like this.

[*He begins to dance. There is no music, only the tortured rhythm of the flogging.* BB *and* MEBUDE *watch him in bemused astonishment. Finally* BB *can no longer take it. He jumps up.* KAMORU *stops dancing and heads towards the door. He pauses at the door.*]

Watch out for that dance, BB,
for those steps. It means—
You want me to tell you what it means?
It means the game was good,
the haul was great, and the prey
—the prey ran out of luck.
And God simply watches.

Scene Three

A moment later. Another remand cell in the courthouse.

YINKA is slumped over a chair, bloodied up, a tape across his lips. He is breathing hoarsely. There is little life left in him.

An OLD WOMAN enters the room. She is bathed in a shower of light. She undoes the tape across his lips.

OLD WOMAN I heard you
calling out for help.
I heard your voice reaching out to me.

YINKA [*with disbelief*] Mother?

OLD WOMAN I heard your screams,
your cries.
I felt every stroke
that hit your body,
every pain that you felt.

YINKA Is this heaven—or hell? Am I dead?

OLD WOMAN You have been
a naughty son, Yinka.
Even where I was,
I bent my head with shame.
I was covered in shame.
What did I do wrong as a mother?
I tried to bring you up well.

[*He holds her like a baby, shaking with emotion.*]

YINKA I tried, mother, I tried.

[INSPECTOR KAMORU *enters, followed by a female* DOCTOR. *They do not see the* OLD WOMAN.]

I'm sorry, mother. You must forgive me.

[*He slumps back into the chair.*]

ACT TWO

KAMORU He's in a delirium. He's been calling out to his mother all day. I knew the woman, you know, doctor. I was going to say she would be turning in her grave if she knew what her son had turned into. But that would be rather rich coming from her. She wasn't herself exactly a pinnacle of rectitude, you see. At the height of her career, she was the most sought-after good-time woman from Shomolu to Bariga.

[*The* OLD WOMAN *clouts* KAMORU *on the side of the face. He turns round sharply, smarting with pain.*]

[*to* DOCTOR] That was infantile and uncalled for. If you don't like what I'm saying, just say so and I'll shut up. That's why God gave us mouths.

DOCTOR Sorry?

KAMORU Don't say 'sorry'. I hate it when people say 'sorry'. If you know you're going to be sorry, why do it in the first place? [*to himself*] God, I hate it when people say 'sorry'.

DOCTOR There's something going on in your head, Inspector, and I'm not sure I know what it is. [*examining* YINKA's *bloodied head*] Major injuries. Your boys have gone too far this time, Inspector. See that soft, white tissue there? That's his brain. You've split open this man's head.

OLD WOMAN You will have to be strong, Yinka. But it will soon be over. You will leave the pain behind.

YINKA I don't want to die, mother. I don't want to die.

KAMORU What are his chances, doctor?

DOCTOR Precious little, I'm afraid. He's hanging on, just about. Even if we do manage to keep him alive, he'll require care for the rest of his life. We do not have facilities for that. I shall send for an ambulance. And, Inspector, there'll be a very thorough inquest. I shall see to that.

KAMORU Doctor?

DOCTOR [*very unfriendly*] Yes, Inspector?

[KAMORU *slaps her sharply on the face.*]

KAMORU Fair's fair.

[*The* DOCTOR *leaves, stunned.*]

OLD WOMAN I'm here with you, Yinka.
I shall stay by you all the way.
I shall be holding your hands
when you step across that threshold.

Scene Four

The following morning. Chief Justice BASSEY's *chambers.*

BASSEY *is coming to the end of a conversation on the telephone.*

BASSEY [*on the phone*] Okay, Akunakuna. Okay. You'll tell her to ring me. Won't you? When she comes back? Okay. Okay.

[*He replaces the handset and pours himself a brandy. He observes his guest,* ADAMA, *for a long while.*]

Ms Lawal—?

ADAMA [*leaning forward expectantly*] Your honour?

BASSEY Have you ever suspected your husband of cheating on you?

[*Pause.*]

ADAMA Yes. I mean, hypothetically, that is, seeing as ...

BASSEY [*categorically*] I believe my wife is cheating on me ...

ADAMA ... I do not have a husband.

ACT TWO

BASSEY She's... [*clears his throat*] ...much younger than me, you see.

ADAMA Yes, yes.

>[*Awkward silence.*]

Your honour—?

BASSEY [*absentmindedly*] Rejuvenation, I said. Fresh blood...

ADAMA Your honour, sir?

>[BASSEY *snaps out of it.*]

BASSEY Are you going to sit there all day looking like a prize fool?

ADAMA I, your honour...

BASSEY [*curtly*] I received quite a number of phone calls last night. From the General's office, the state governor, the minister of justice. You know about these, don't you?

ADAMA Vaguely, your honour, vaguely.

BASSEY To put it squarely and precisely: all these people—the General, the governor, the justice minister—have been getting up my nose over your client's case. They've been—most reprehensibly, I must say—getting up my nose over the case of Mr Babarinsa. [*Pause.*] Do you know what I do when I've got something up my nose, Ms Lawal?

ADAMA You get a handkerchief, sir?

>[*Pause.*]

BASSEY No. I pick it.

>[*Pause.*]

I pick it and see if I can flick it to the ceiling.

>[ADAMA *looks suspiciously up at the ceiling.*]

That's what I wanted to do to the General, and the governor, and the minister. However...

> [*He picks up the framed picture of the boy on his desk and studies it as he speaks.*]

I've given it lengthy thought, all night.

> [*He pours another large shot of brandy. He offers to pour one for* ADAMA *as well; she declines, preferring instead to light a cigarette.*]

We're living in very interesting times.

ADAMA That's a Chinese curse, sir.

BASSEY What?

ADAMA 'May you live in interesting times.'

> [BASSEY *downs the brandy and pours himself another shot.*]

BASSEY [*absently, not paying any heed to* ADAMA] We're living in very interesting times. And we all have to live. As best we can.

> [*He pours another shot. Pause.*]

How much are you offering?

> [ADAMA *sits still for another moment, considering the best response. She gestures at pen and paper.* BASSEY *scribbles on a sheet of paper and slides it across to her.*]

We're not here to haggle.

> [*Pause.*]

ADAMA [*slowly*] What about half of this—half a million naira?

BASSEY A million. Or, I'm sorry to say...

ADAMA [*with a feigned tone of finality*] Half a million, your honour. London or Geneva account?

> [*Pause. Then* BASSEY *capitulates.*]

BASSEY Alright, then, half a million. Cash.

ADAMA I'm afraid—

BASSEY [*emphatically*] Cash.

[*Pause.*]

ADAMA [*finally*] And, erhm, BB will walk free? Today?

BASSEY Today. I've almost finished writing the summing up.

[*Pause.*]

Cash. I want it all in cash.

ADAMA [*hardly able to conceal her excitement*] Of course, your honour.

[*She pulls up a briefcase from the floor beside her, and slides it across the table.* BASSEY *clicks it open.*]

BASSEY I trust you.

[*He clicks the briefcase shut and deals out brandy into two glasses.*]

ADAMA [*accepting a glass of brandy*] Your honour: to justice.

[*They clink glasses.*]

BASSEY By the way, when is that client of yours going to make an honest woman of my daughter? Of course, I use the word honest rather guardedly in this instance. In inverted commas.

[*They laugh.*]

Scene Five

Later that morning. Inside the courtroom, where the court is in session. From outside we hear the incessant beating of talking drums and a singing troupe, but principally the voices of the BEGGARS.

BB *is standing, not in the dock, but with* ADAMA, MEBUDE *and* SANTANA *sitting beside him. They are dressed in resplendent, celebratory dresses.*

BASSEY [*sipping from a glass of water*] ...My abiding memory of these last few weeks will be undoubtedly of those scenes outside this court, replayed day after day, when crowds have gathered to express their admiration for Mr Babarinsa. Certain sections of the media have dismissed this as being merely symptomatic of the degenerate climes in which we live: an amoral state of affairs where all symbols of social subversion—criminality even—are deified, worshipped. I choose to see it differently. Mr Babarinsa attracts such love and loyalty, not only because of his God-given charisma, but because he is a jolly good fellow.

[*Applause from* BB's *side of the court. A small smile is betrayed on* BB's *features.*]

Mr Babarinsa is without doubt an inestimable asset to the nation.

[*Applause.*]

I have no doubt in my mind that if we had ten other minds in our midst today, approaching his in quality of giftedness, we would be back on our feet in no time.

[*Applause.*]

It is because of the above reasons, amongst others, that I find it an immensely difficult decision, having been led by all the evidence that has been presented to this court, to reach a verdict on Bikan Babarinsa—

[*Strained silence in court as he pauses.*]

Of guilty as charged.

[*Deathly silence. Utter disbelief.*]

End of Act Two

Act Three

IN THE HOUR OF THE TRICKSTER-GOD

Scene One

Several days later. Chief Justice BASSEY's *chambers. After court hours.*

BASSEY *is on the telephone. We hear the voices of* BEGGARS *on the street singing a dirge.*

BEGGARS [*singing*] Ile lo loooo
Tarara
Ile lo loooo
Tarara
Baba BB re le re
Ile lo loooo
Tarara*

BASSEY [*on the phone*] Hello Akunakuna... Is that you Akunakuna? Yes. Get me Madam on the line. Yes. I think I might be late coming home tonight. I'd like to have a word with her.

[*A haunted-looking* ADAMA *enters.* BASSEY *waves her to a seat.*]

ADAMA All I want is an explanation.

BASSEY [*on the phone*] She's where? Alright, I'll wait. Go and call her. [*to* ADAMA] Good afternoon, Ms Lawal. I'd been hoping you might drop by one of these days.

---

* He's gone home / he's gone straight home / Baba BB's gone straight home ...

ADAMA I had to sneak in here. My life's in danger. Lunatics are going round Lagos with guns and machetes looking for me. They think I did a Judas on BB. Sooner or later one of them is bound to find me. I thought I deserved an explanation before that happened.

> [BASSEY *pours out two glasses of brandy. He offers one to* ADAMA, *who ignores it.*]

You had a change of mind, is that it? Is that it?

BASSEY [*on the phone*] Hello? Hello? [*to* ADAMA] Have a drink, Ms Lawal. It's good for the nerves. Are you attending the execution? If you are, I hope you've had a seat reserved. I hear they're expecting such a crowd they've decided to charge for entry.

ADAMA What was it, hunh? You ... You ...

> [*She moves threateningly towards* BASSEY. BASSEY *downs his drink.*]

BASSEY [*pressing a security call button on the desk*] I wouldn't do anything naughty if I were you, Ms Lawal.

> [*Two* SECURITY MEN *come in. They seize* ADAMA *by the arms.* BASSEY *signals for them to wait.*]

ADAMA [*struggling ineffectually*] I—I don't understand at all. I don't understand this game of yours.

BASSEY I do not play games, Ms Lawal. And if you know anything about our culture, you'll realise that it is bad manners to turn down a gift. Out of the kindness of your heart you offered me a gift. I took the gift. I was grateful for that gift.

ADAMA A gift? [*screaming*] A gift? Are you fucking insane. A g—

BASSEY I do not take kindly to swearing in my chambers.

ADAMA A gift? A gift? You're out of your mind, I tell you. That was a bribe, you little man! A bribe, you idiot ...!

ACT THREE

[*From outside the courthouse the* BEGGARS' *singing rises.*]

BEGGARS [*off*] Ile lo loooo
Tarara
Ile lo loooo
Baba BB re le re
Ile lo loooo
Tarara.

BASSEY [*to* ADAMA] They do not sound amused. I can see that you're not amused either. [*to the* SECURITY MEN] Kindly deposit the lady outside the gates, please. She's got friends waiting for her.

[*They manhandle* ADAMA *out.*]

[BASSEY *picks up the photograph of his son. He wipes it clean with a handkerchief. He picks up another framed photograph from the desk. It is* MEBUDE *in her graduation gown. He hangs both photographs on the wall. He picks up the telephone.*]

[*on the phone*] Hello? Akunakuna? Yes? [*impatiently*] Yes, yes. I beg your pardon! Do you know who is speaking? So you... are you there... you idiot child! Get me my wife on the line this very moment. You what? [*Pause.*] I'm not used to being disobeyed, Akunakuna. I seldom suffer fools gladly. You'll notice that my voice quakes, ever so slightly. That means that I am getting angry. Very angry. Get me my wife this very moment! This very moment! Now!

[*The response from the other end nearly makes him yank the cord off from the telephone.*]

[*on the phone*] *Whaaaaat?* Did I hear you right? Did you say she was in the bedroom with someone? [*Pause. Deep breath.*] Are you sure? [*Pause.*] Are you absolutely—? [*Long pause.*] Akunakuna? Oh my... Listen, Akunakuna. Are you listening?

> [*He pours a large brandy and knocks it down in one go.*]

[*on the phone*] I have a proposition for you. It's worth... [*Short reflective pause.*] ... half a million. Yes, Akunakuna. Half a million. Cash. This is all you've got to do. Go to the guest room and check the wardrobe there. You'll find a brown oilskin briefcase with a broken handle. Inside you'll find a pistol... [*Pause to listen to reaction. Safe.*] It's in a drawer in the library, not the guest room? Is that so? I know it's there somewhere. Get it. Get it and shoot them both. Yes, that's what I said. Shoot them both, the shameless woman and her lover. Half a million naira. Cash. Yes... I'll hold on.

> [*As he holds on, he presses a button on the portable tape recorder on his desk. Louis Armstrong's* A Kiss To Build A Dream On *comes blasting forth. He whistles and croons to it. In the distance a series of gunshots goes off.*]

[*on the phone*] Erm, yes. Akunakuna. Yes. Good. Good. That's my boy. Now take their bodies out and dump them in the disused swimming pool. [*Pause.*] Yes, the swimming pool. What do you mean, which swimming pool? How many swimming pools—? [*Pause.*] There is no swimming pool there? [*He picks up the brandy and takes a swig. Pause.*] Is that really you, Akunakuna....? Thank God. For one horrible moment I thought... Is this 88 88 87? [*Long pause.*] No? It is... [*slowly*] 88 88 89. [*He stares blankly ahead of him.*] Oh my God.

> [*He drops the phone and takes another swig from the brandy.*]

Oh my God.

Scene Two

Later that day.

A football field that has been converted into an execution ground by the simple expedient of placing in its middle an oil drum stacked with bags of sand.

BB is led to the stake by two uniformed SOLDIERS. As he is being tied to the drum, he waves casually to a mixture of applause and abuse from a screaming crowd out of sight. The SOLDIERS are armed with standard army rifles.

MEBUDE and SANTANA watch. INSPECTOR KAMORU looks on. The DOCTOR in attendance observes, expressionless. Outside of our view, the BEGGARS' dirge.

BB [*to one of the* SOLDIERS] Do I know you?

   [*The* SOLDIER, *a teenager, ignores him and studiously continues strapping the rope around him.*]

   Do I know you, boy?

   [*The* SOLDIER *stiffens.*]

   Do I—?

SOLDIER 1 Don't call me boy.

SOLDIER 2 [*to* SOLDIER 1] Come on, Bas, the man's about to die. The least you could say is thank you.

SOLDIER 1 Stay out of this, will you? [*shouts*] Will you stay out of this!

SOLDIER 2 Come on, Bas...

SOLDIER 1 Will you!

SOLDIER 2 [*to himself*] Jesus, I hate ingrates.

MEBUDE [*to* BB] I know him. His mother had a stall by the Junction. She came to you once—I was there—she was all tears. Her stall had been broken into, she had no money, her son was about to be kicked out of school...

SOLDIER 1 I de warn you, Madam, I'm ready to go to jail for you.

[*They finish tying up* BB.]

[*to* BB, *quietly*] Just because you helped my mother out once does not mean...a thing. It doesn't, you hear me? You hear me!

SANTANA He didn't just help your mother out, he gave you a scholarship.

[SOLDIER 1 *strikes* SANTANA.]

SOLDIER 1 [*to* BB] I want you to know that I volunteered for this. I asked for this job.

BB Just out of curiosity—why?

SOLDIER 1 Why? I should be asking you that question.

BB I was well brought up.
I was taught as a child to
always answer a question.
You see, I looked to greatness
when I was a child.
I lived in a world that had seven doors—

SANTANA [*on cue*] One for luck,
one for joy,
one for coming,
one for going,
one for friends,
one for foes,
and one that opened
into a fiery abyss.

BB I dreamed of greatness
when I was a child.
I dreamed dreams,
Created beauty,

SANTANA Sang songs in smiling sleeps.

BB But with growing up
came my undoing.
I loved too much—

ACT THREE 69

SANTANA —and choked the dreams in my heart,

BB I hated much more—

SANTANA —and drowned the visions in my head.

BB With growing up
came my undoing.
I lived many dreams but none was mine.
I got kicked once—

SANTANA —where it hurts.

BB And my eyes cleared
—watered at first,
and then cleared—
I saw the light.

SANTANA But it wasn't green.

BB The mist cleared,
the fog disappeared,
the headlights of a car
caught me in the face.
I felt like a space
trapped between walls.
I wiped my face
and discovered—

SANTANA —too late—

BB —it wasn't the sweat
I'd wiped off but a
smile that was being born.
I punched the air
in a dance of joy,
then felt like a fool—

SANTANA —it was the wrong response.

SOLDIER 1 [*nonplussed*] Right. Right. [*collecting his thoughts*] You wanted to know why I volunteered for this? This is why: without scum like you around, I wouldn't have needed a scholarship from you in the first place.

BB You're wrong, soldier. You should be pointing that gun at the people who placed it in your hands.

KAMORU Ready!

> [*The* SOLDIERS *salute and then march to their positions.* MEBUDE *steps forward and hugs* BB. SOLDIER 1 *comes over to pull* MEBUDE *away. She shakes him off and leaves. The* SOLDIERS *take position and fire at* BB. *He slumps. His body is taken away.*]

> [*As all this is happening,* SANTANA *steps forward and addresses the audience.*]

SANTANA [*accompanied by the throbbings of a talking drum*] And so ended the earthly journey of Baba BB, King of Ketu. Such was his fame, such the draw of his name, that on the day of his execution the whole of Ketu came out, in their tens of thousands, to witness the event and to pay their last respects. To honour his memory, the thieves and burglars of Ketu embarked on a campaign the like of which had never been known before. For three weeks not a day passed without whole streets being broken into, banks being held up, cars being seized in broad daylight. The police mourned him by going unannounced on industrial action, so that while more crimes were recorded during those three weeks than for the entire year that had just gone by, not a single arrest was made. In some neighbourhoods, Happy Hours were declared: everybody was free to break into their neighbours' and take whatever they could, without fear of retribution. You see, so many people had depended on BB for a living. His execution was like the closure of a major factory in an industrial town. Such was the sadness, such the anger that once again the government had surpassed itself in shortcircuiting the hopes of the people while remaining unable and, in any case, unwilling to help them out.

I, Santana, who sat down with your story-teller and over several gourds of wine and countless pieces of cola-nut, told him this unfolding tale. I had left Ketu by this time, and only tell this from hearsay. It will take too long to go into what happened to me after the death of BB. Suffice it to say that I went on to prosper in life. I went back to my village. Got married to the blacksmith's daughter, Ibukun, who had golden gaps between her teeth, and in her eyes, flames that rose like smoke in the forest-burning months of harmattan. And when she smiled, you smiled with her. To be unhappy in Ibukun's presence was something many tried but could never quite achieve. Of her beauty songs were written. The highways and village paths were littered with hearts broken by Ibukun the blacksmith's daughter. And yet— [*Pause.*] —she chose me. We had children. Many children. And later on, much later on, grandchildren. By this time I was approaching my seventieth year, and in the second dawn of my life. Once in a while, when the mood came upon me, and my tongue was eased with wine, I would wrench my grandchildren from their parents and from their computer games and I would tell them the story of the King of Ketu. And of my grandfather's visits from the grave. Always, when I told them these stories, I would set out to tell the truth, to recount the tales as I remembered them. But memory is a trickster-god. It promises shifting sands but plunges you into shallow waters. And then breaks out in a wide grin as it pulls you out, all soaked-out but the wiser for it. And so, night after night, my grandchildren would indulge me as I regaled them with the life of Baba

BB—gangster, lover, philanthropist. I told them of lives wasted, of talents misused, opportunities misspent. But just so they would go to bed happy—for they did not like a tale with a sad ending—I would give the story a twist in its tail. I would give it a different ending. A happy ending. Or rather, the ending that *I* would have wished. Here. See for yourself. [*Pause.*] Once upon a time...

[*Talking drums.*]

End of Act Three

Epilogue

IN THE SEASON OF THE LONGEST DROUGHT

A time in the future. The street.

A crowd of townspeople, including the BEGGARS, *are gathered under a huge Iroko tree, listening to a man. The man is naked save for a pair of shorts improvised from palm fronds. His hair is mangy, as if it has never come into contact with a comb. It is* BB.

BB A long time ago, there was a drought in Ketu. Seven harvests and seven harmattans and not one drop of rain. The farmlands dried up, plants withered, the streams boiled and went up in smoke, oceans turned into rocks and emitted fire, the moon disappeared, eaten up by the sun. The sun moved closer to earth and people melted under its gaze. No-one knew what to do. Not the elders, nor the priests, nor the guardians of the deities' words. At last the people of Ketu, those few still alive, and the birds of the air and the beasts of the land and the inhabitants of the wild brought their heads together, determined to find a solution.

They decided to send a messenger to the Gods, a supplicant to Olodumare, the creator. But Olodumare lived far away, in the skies, beyond the clouds, beyond the sun, beyond a place where no-one had ever been before. One way or the other, someone had to go. They decided to choose this emissary by lot and it fell on man. But man refused to go, saying he couldn't fly. Another lot was cast and it fell on the tortoise. But he too refused to go, pleading his lack of speed.

At last, the vulture stood up and offered to go. Now the vulture was at this time the most loathed of birds; she was only to be found where there had been a death. Some grumbled but would not themselves volunteer, and so finally the vulture was sent off with the errand. She froze in the clouds and was burned by the sun, but such was her will she let nothing stand in her way. It took her several moons but she got there in the end. She delivered the offering and headed back to earth.

Olodumare relented and granted rain. The vulture herself was caught in it. By the time she set foot on Ketu she was cold and wet and miserable. She went to the first house she saw to seek shelter from the rain and warmth from the cold. But the owners of the house shut their door in her face. Sorry, they said, but you're dripping with water, we do not want our carpet wet. She went from door to door all over the town and, for the same reason, no-one would let her in.

BEGGAR 1 I have but one question, sir, and it's very profound.

BB Yes, blind friend?

BEGGAR 1 My question is—and I mean no disrespect—doesn't that carpet at the end of your story smack of taking literary licence to absurd extents?

BB What have we here—an educated beggar or a cynical blind man?

BEGGAR 2 Six of one, and half a dozen of the other. Since he learned to use a braille machine he has grabbed every chance to show off his brilliance, his claim to wit, his erudition, his grasp of logic—most of it, to wit, rather dim, if you'll pardon the pun.

BB Step forward, friend. Were you born blind?

BEGGAR 1 Some are born blind, some acquire blindness and some have blindness thrust upon them. I belong to the last group, sir. I used to be a man of, shall we say, questionable character—

BEGGAR 2 A drug dealer.

BB I've been there too, friend.

BEGGAR 1 I ran into certain difficulties—

BEGGAR 3 He tried to do a runner with money that didn't belong to him—

BEGGAR 1 A merely human impulse, sir. Next thing I knew, two men pounced on me in this very street and took knives to my eyes.

BEGGAR 2 I saw it happen, sir. Since then I haven't been able to stand the sight of an omelette. And we've been stuck with him ever since.

BB Well, blind man, open your eyes and walk away.

BEGGAR 1 I believe you're trying to run even before you can crawl, sir. May I refer you to the example of the man who holds a copyright on those words. He tested his wand first by turning water into wine.

BB [*to* BEGGAR 1] I said, open your eyes and walk away.

[BEGGAR 1 *shrugs, rubs his eyes and opens them. He can see. He stands absolutely stock still and begins to scream.*]

BEGGAR 1 I can see! I can see! I can see!

[ADAMA *appears. She is in rags.*]

ADAMA I'm looking for Judge Bassey. Does anyone know Judge Bassey?

BB Adama. Is this you, Adama?

BEGGAR 3   [*leaning forward*] You mean to say you know her?

ADAMA   I'm looking for Judge Bassey. Does anyone know Judge Bassey?

   [*She leaves.*]

BEGGAR 1   Looks like you're meeting everyone today, sir. That was the town loony. She used to be a lawyer.

ADAMA   [*off*] I'm looking for Judge Bassey. Does anyone know Judge Bassey?

   [JUDGE BASSEY *appears. He looks tattered, the worse for wear. He sees* BB *and blinks in recognition and disbelief.*]

BASSEY   Thank God, I'm finally losing my mind. Or why else do I think you look like—in fact, that you are—a fellow who was executed very close to this very spot in the now distant past.

BEGGAR 1   'In the now distant past.' Why can't you just say 'long ago'?

BB   I've been looking for you, Judge Bassey—

BEGGAR 3   [*to* BEGGAR 1] He knows his name!

BB   [*to* BASSEY] —where have you been?

BASSEY   [*to himself*] Oh God, this must be a sign from God. [*to* BB] I've, erm, been away.

BEGGAR 1   At the government's pleasure. We shared a cell once at Yaba prison.

BASSEY   Pinch me, someone. I know this is a dream.

BEGGAR 2   [*viciously pinching him*] No, it's not, you plonker.

BEGGAR 1   [*to* BB] Do you really know him?

BB   He was my executioner, and father-in-law-to-be.

BEGGAR 2   And I suppose you're a joker. To-be. If he was your father-in-law-to-be, then *she* must've been your bride-to-be.

BB   Who?

BEGGAR 2   This tree under which we stand.

EPILOGUE

BEGGAR 1   This Iroko under which we stand. It happened before I lost my sight. One morning, the judge's daughter—

BB/BEGGAR 1   —Ebun.

BEGGAR 1   —yes, how did you know her name? It was shortly after her lover, BB—

BEGGAR 2   'King of Ketu', we used to call him—

BEGGAR 3   —faced the firing squad and went down like a man—

BEGGAR 2   —shouting 'Up yours', to the very last.

BEGGAR 1   She was travelling abroad on some trifle or another—

BEGGAR 2   —a summer holiday.

BEGGAR 1   She was on her way to the airport to catch a flight. She took her car.

BEGGAR 2   There was a mango tree here then. Old, and no longer bearing fruit. Her brake failed—

BEGGAR 1   —someone tampered with it.

BEGGAR 2   No-one tampered with it. Your love for intrigue sometimes wearies me. Her brake failed and she drove straight into the tree. She died instantly.

BEGGAR 1   Next thing we knew, when we woke up the following day, the mango tree had disappeared. In its place stood this Iroko.

BEGGAR 3   He came to her once, after he was blinded.

BEGGAR 1   I went on my knees, right on this spot. 'Please restore my sight', I pleaded.

BEGGAR 2   'Piss off' came the response.

BEGGAR 1   I swear it was her voice I heard.

BEGGAR 2   That was when he started to lose his faith. I'd read to him from the Bible and he'd say—

BEGGAR 1   'Oh put that thing away, woman.'

BEGGAR 2   'It's not a thing, it's the Holy Book.'

BEGGAR 1 'That's not a book, just a lot of fancy designs with a bubble-jet printer.'

BB You do fancy yourselves comedians, don't you?

BEGGAR 1 By the grace of God, it's our calling. We make people laugh, sir, through the wrong hole in their face.

BEGGARS 2 / 3 It's called sneezing.

BEGGAR 1 We make people laugh, sir, and they go away blowing their nose.

BEGGARS 2 / 3 It's called crying.

BEGGAR 1 We make people laugh, sir, so they may never laugh again.

BEGGARS 2 / 3 It's called inoculation.

BASSEY Is this really you, BB?

BEGGAR 1 [*to* BEGGAR 2] Did he say BB? [*slaps* BB, *half-mockingly*] Get away!

BB Yes, Judge Bassey. I've returned. I've been sent to clean up some of the mess around here. There was a population explosion up there. Too many souls dying before their time—

BEGGAR 1 You've restored my sight, sir, but there's more to this than meets the eye.

BB The Big One up there hit on the perfect solution: send back the buggers to clean up the mess themselves. Which suited me fine. I missed you guys. If you go round the corner this very moment and into the next street, you'll find a young man, Dele, who went of an overdose.

BASSEY Dele? My boy?

BB The very same. Go round the corner and you'll find him talking to another gathering similar to this.

BASSEY [*kneeling down*] Thank you, O Lord, for allowing me to be a witness to the Second Coming.

EPILOGUE

[*He runs off, shouting.*]

Dele! Dele! Dele!

BEGGAR 1 [*to* BEGGAR 2] Does that mean that he's—?

BEGGAR 2 I'm willing to bet my last Kobo on it.

BEGGAR 1 This can't be real. This is Kafka—on speed!

[BEGGAR 1 *brings out a fairly big crucifix from his gown and peers at it.*]

BEGGAR 1 [*whispers to* BEGGAR 2] I don't see much of a resemblance.

BEGGAR 3 Perhaps he shaved the beard?

BEGGAR 1 And got a suntan as well?

BEGGAR 2 Christ is black, you idiot.

BEGGAR 1 Christ had a tan?

BEGGARS 2/3 Shut up.

[*They kneel.*]

BEGGARS Thank you, O Lord, for allowing us to be witnesses to Your Second Coming.

[YINKA *appears. The* BEGGARS *see him, whisper to themselves and turn to look at him, visibly surprised. He is closely followed by* INSPECTOR KAMORU *in tattered police uniform. A strong wind blows through. A feast of leaves falls from the Iroko tree and covers the townspeople.*]

BB Get up, you all. I didn't say I was Christ. He is still in a daze, by the way. What you have here is an invasion of vultures. And we've been empowered to kick down doors. We've got a mandate to cleanse and—if necessary—to kick arse. In this season of the longest drought, the messengers will not be crucified.

[*It begins to rain. Thunder and lightning. Lights fade to black.*]

The End